Rhyming
on the Road

By Kathleen Connors

Gareth Stevens
Publishing

Please visit our website, www.garethstevens.com. For a free color catalog of all our high-quality books, call toll free 1-800-542-2595 or fax 1-877-542-2596.

Library of Congress Cataloging-in-Publication Data

Connors, Kathleen.
Rhyming on the road / Kathleen Connors.
    p. cm. — (Word play)
Includes index.
ISBN 978-1-4339-7200-3 (pbk.)
ISBN 978-1-4339-7201-0 (6-pack)
ISBN 978-1-4339-7199-0 (library binding) –
1. English language—Rhyme—Juvenile literature. I. Title.
PE1517.C66 2012
808.1—dc23
                                    2011051765

First Edition

Published in 2013 by
Gareth Stevens Publishing
111 East 14th Street, Suite 349
New York, NY 10003

Copyright © 2013 Gareth Stevens Publishing

Designer: Benjamin Gardner
Editor: Kristen Rajczak

Photo credits: Cover, p. 1 Robert Asento/Shutterstock.com; p. 5 Kurhan/Shutterstock.com; p. 7 Symbiot/Shutterstock.com; p. 9 Suzanne Tucker/Shutterstock.com; p. 11 Gorilla/Shutterstock.com; p. 13 bikeriderlondon/Shutterstock.com; p. 15 wavebreakmedia ltd/Shutterstock.com; p. 17 Gorilla/Shutterstock.com; p. 19 © iStockphoto.com/digitalskillet.

Printed in the United States of America

CPSIA compliance information: Batch #CS12GS: For further information contact Gareth Stevens, New York, New York at 1-800-542-2595.

Contents

Boldface words appear in the glossary.

Let's Go!

Hurry up! We have places to go. We're hopping in the **car** and driving somewhere **far** away.

Say **car** and **far** out loud. Do they sound the same? That's because **car** and **far** rhyme!

5

What Is Rhyme?

Words that rhyme have matching sounds. That means the last part of one word sounds like the last part of another word.

Drivers know to **go slow** when the road is wet.

Go and **slow** have the same long "o" sound. They rhyme!

7

Show Me the Money

We're on our **way**! Did you bring a few dollars? Sometimes, cars and trucks have to **pay** a **toll** when they use a road.

Way and **pay** have a matching long "a" sound. They're rhyming words!

STOP AHEAD PAY TOLL

CASH ONLY
LEFT LANES

CARS ONLY ALL VEHICLES

9

Finding the Way

Use a **map** to find your way on the road. It shows you how far apart places are and what roads to take. If it's a long trip, you might take a **nap**.

Say **map** and **nap** out loud. They rhyme.

Break Time

Have you ever been in a car all day? It's so nice when you get out to **stretch** your legs. It's even better if you get to run and **play** for a little while!

Day and **play** have a matching sound. They rhyme!

Food on the Go

Many families pack **lunch** when they take car trips. It might include sandwiches, a **bunch** of grapes, or other snacks.

Lunch and **bunch** share sounds and are spelled alike. Many rhyming words have spellings that are close to one another.

Pack Up

Time to get back on the **road**! **Load** up the **picnic** supplies and toys. We don't want to leave anything behind.

Do **road** and **load** rhyme? Say them out loud. They do!

Are We There Yet?

A car **game** can help pass the time while traveling. **Name** all the different **license plates** you see. **Game** and **name** rhyme!

We're Here!

Some car rides are short. Your mom might drive you down the **street** to **meet** a friend.

Do **meet** and **street** rhyme? Say them out loud to make sure!

Common Rhyming Words

food $\rightarrow$ mood

run $\rightarrow$ fun $\rightarrow$ sun

side $\rightarrow$ wide

walk $\rightarrow$ talk

shoe $\rightarrow$ chew $\rightarrow$ blue

park $\rightarrow$ dark

Glossary

license plate: metal plates on the front and back of a car that tell where the car is from

picnic: an outdoor meal

stretch: to lengthen

toll: a payment made to use a road

For More Information

Books

Thomas, Jan. *Rhyming Dust Bunnies.* New York, NY: Atheneum Books for Young Readers, 2009.

Wheeler, Lisa. *The Pet Project: Cute and Cuddly Vicious Verses.* New York, NY: Atheneum Books for Young Readers, 2013.

Websites

Rhyming Games

pbskids.org/games/rhyming.html

Play games to practice rhyming words.

Speakaboos: Nursery Rhymes

www.speakaboos.com/theme/nursery-rhymes

Listen to common nursery rhymes and watch videos.

Index